The Key Facts™ on

Pakistan

Essential Information on Pakistan

By Patrick W. Nee

The Internationalist®

www.internationalist.com

The Internationalist®

International Business, Investment, and Travel

Published by:

The Internationalist Publishing Company

96 Walter Street/ Suite 200

Boston, MA 02131, USA

Tel: 617-354-7722

www.internationalist.com

PN@internationalist.com

Table Of Contents

Chapter 1: Background

The Indus Valley civilization, one of the oldest in the world and dating back at least 5,000 years, spread over much of what is presently Pakistan. During the second millennium B.C., remnants of this culture fused with the migrating Indo-Aryan peoples. The area underwent successive invasions in subsequent centuries from the Persians, Greeks, Scythians, Arabs (who brought Islam), Afghans, and Turks. The Mughal Empire flourished in the 16th and 17th centuries; the British came to dominate the region in the 18th century. The separation in 1947 of British India into the Muslim state of Pakistan (with West and East sections) and largely Hindu India was never satisfactorily resolved, and India and Pakistan fought two wars - in 1947-48 and 1965 - over the disputed Kashmir territory. A third war between these countries in 1971 - in which India capitalized on Islamabad's marginalization of Bengalis in Pakistani politics - resulted in East Pakistan becoming the separate nation of Bangladesh. In response to Indian nuclear weapons testing, Pakistan conducted its own tests in 1998. India-Pakistan relations have been rocky since the November 2008 Mumbai attacks, but both countries are taking small steps to put relations back on track. In February 2008, Pakistan held parliamentary elections and in September 2008, after the resignation of former President MUSHARRAF, elected Asif Ali ZARDARI to the presidency. Pakistani government and military leaders are struggling to control domestic insurgents, many of whom are located in the tribal areas adjacent to the border with Afghanistan. In January 2012, Pakistan assumed a nonpermanent seat on the UN Security Council for the 2012-13 term.

Chapter 2: Geography

Location:

> Southern Asia, bordering the Arabian Sea, between India on the east and Iran and Afghanistan on the west and China in the north

Geographic coordinates:

> 30 00 N, 70 00 E

Map references:

> Asia

Area:

> total: 796,095 sq km
>
> country comparison to the world: 36
>
> land: 770,875 sq km
>
> water: 25,220 sq km

Area - comparative:

> slightly less than twice the size of California

Land boundaries:

> total: 6,774 km
>
> border countries: Afghanistan 2,430 km, China 523 km, India 2,912 km, Iran 909 km

Coastline:

> 1,046 km

Maritime claims:

> territorial sea: 12 nm
>
> contiguous zone: 24 nm

exclusive economic zone: 200 nm

continental shelf: 200 nm or to the edge of the continental margin

Climate:

mostly hot, dry desert; temperate in northwest; arctic in north

Terrain:

flat Indus plain in east; mountains in north and northwest; Balochistan plateau in west

Elevation extremes:

lowest point: Indian Ocean 0 m

highest point: K2 (Mt. Godwin-Austen) 8,611 m

Natural resources:

land, extensive natural gas reserves, limited petroleum, poor quality coal, iron ore, copper, salt, limestone

Land use:

arable land: 24.44%

permanent crops: 0.84%

other: 74.72% (2005)

Irrigated land:

198,700 sq km (2003)

Total renewable water resources:

233.8 cu km (2003)

Freshwater withdrawal (domestic/industrial/agricultural):

total: 169.39 cu km/yr (2%/2%/96%)

per capita: 1,072 cu m/yr (2000)

Natural hazards:

> frequent earthquakes, occasionally severe especially in north and west; flooding along the Indus after heavy rains (July and August)

Environment - current issues:

> water pollution from raw sewage, industrial wastes, and agricultural runoff; limited natural freshwater resources; most of the population does not have access to potable water; deforestation; soil erosion; desertification

Environment - international agreements:

> party to: Biodiversity, Climate Change, Climate Change-Kyoto Protocol, Desertification, Endangered Species, Environmental Modification, Hazardous Wastes, Law of the Sea, Marine Dumping, Ozone Layer Protection, Ship Pollution, Wetlands
>
> signed, but not ratified: Marine Life Conservation

Geography - note:

> controls Khyber Pass and Bolan Pass, traditional invasion routes between Central Asia and the Indian Subcontinent

Chapter 3: People and Society

Nationality:

noun: Pakistani(s)

adjective: Pakistani

Ethnic groups:

Punjabi 44.68%, Pashtun (Pathan) 15.42%, Sindhi 14.1%, Sariaki 8.38%, Muhajirs 7.57%, Balochi 3.57%, other 6.28%

Languages:

Punjabi 48%, Sindhi 12%, Saraiki (a Punjabi variant) 10%, Pashtu 8%, Urdu (official) 8%, Balochi 3%, Hindko 2%, Brahui 1%, English (official; lingua franca of Pakistani elite and most government ministries), Burushaski, and other 8%

Religions:

Muslim (official) 96.4% (Sunni 85-90%, Shia 10-15%), other (includes Christian and Hindu) 3.6% (2010 est.)

Population:

190,291,129 (July 2012 est.)

country comparison to the world: 6

Age structure:

0-14 years: 34.7% (male 33,941,828/female 32,130,001)

15-24 years: 21.7% (male 21,283,907/female 19,951,750)

25-54 years: 34.5% (male 34,171,096/female 31,564,622)

55-64 years: 4.8% (male 4,539,939/female 4,633,292)

<u>65 years and over</u>: 4.2% (male 3,808,536/female 4,266,158) (2012 est.)

Median age:

<u>total</u>: 21.9 years

<u>male</u>: 21.9 years

<u>female</u>: 22 years (2012 est.)

Population growth rate:

1.551% (2012 est.)

<u>country comparison to the world</u>: 77

Birth rate:

24.3 births/1,000 population (2012 est.)

<u>country comparison to the world</u>: 65

Death rate:

6.8 deaths/1,000 population (July 2012 est.)

<u>country comparison to the world</u>: 138

Net migration rate:

-2 migrant(s)/1,000 population (2012 est.)

<u>country comparison to the world</u>: 165

Urbanization:

<u>urban population</u>: 36% of total population (2010)

<u>rate of urbanization</u>: 3.1% annual rate of change (2010-15 est.)

Major cities - population:

Karachi 13.125 million; Lahore 7.132 million; Faisalabad 2.849 million; Rawalpindi 2.026 million; ISLAMABAD (capital) 832,000 (2009)

Sex ratio:

at birth: 1.05 male(s)/female

under 15 years: 1.06 male(s)/female

15-64 years: 1.07 male(s)/female

65 years and over: 0.89 male(s)/female

total population: 1.06 male(s)/female (2011 est.)

Maternal mortality rate:

260 deaths/100,000 live births (2010)

country comparison to the world: 43

Infant mortality rate:

total: 61.27 deaths/1,000 live births

country comparison to the world: 25

male: 64.51 deaths/1,000 live births

female: 57.88 deaths/1,000 live births (2012 est.)

Life expectancy at birth:

total population: 66.35 years

country comparison to the world: 166

male: 64.52 years

female: 68.28 years (2012 est.)

Total fertility rate:

3.07 children born/woman (2012 est.)

country comparison to the world: 59

Health expenditures:

2.6% of GDP (2009)

country comparison to the world: 182

Physicians density:

0.813 physicians/1,000 population (2009)

Hospital bed density:

0.6 beds/1,000 population (2009)

Sanitation facility access:

improved:

urban: 72% of population

rural: 29% of population

total: 45% of population

unimproved:

urban: 28% of population

rural: 71% of population

total: 55% of population

HIV/AIDS - adult prevalence rate:

0.1% (2009 est.)

country comparison to the world: 146

HIV/AIDS - people living with HIV/AIDS:

98,000 (2009 est.)

country comparison to the world: 42

HIV/AIDS - deaths:

5,800 (2009 est.)

country comparison to the world: 34

Major infectious diseases:

degree of risk: high

food or waterborne diseases: bacterial diarrhea, hepatitis A and E, and typhoid fever

vectorborne diseases: dengue fever and malaria

animal contact disease: rabies

note: highly pathogenic H5N1 avian influenza has been identified in this country; it poses a negligible risk with extremely rare cases possible among US citizens who have close contact with birds (2009)

Children under the age of 5 years underweight:

31.3% (2001)

country comparison to the world: 17

Education expenditures:

2.7% of GDP (2009)

country comparison to the world: 142

Literacy:

definition: age 15 and over can read and write

total population: 54.9%

male: 68.6%

female: 40.3% (2009 est.)

School life expectancy (primary to tertiary education):

total: 7 years

male: 8 years

female: 6 years (2009)

Unemployment, youth ages 15-24:

total: 7.7%

country comparison to the world: 114

male: 7%

female: 10.5% (2008)

Chapter 4: Government

Country name:

>conventional long form: Islamic Republic of Pakistan
>
>conventional short form: Pakistan
>
>local long form: Jamhuryat Islami Pakistan
>
>local short form: Pakistan
>
>former: West Pakistan

Government type:

>federal republic

Capital:

>name: Islamabad
>
>geographic coordinates: 33 41 N, 73 03 E
>
>time difference: UTC+5 (10 hours ahead of Washington, DC during Standard Time)

Administrative divisions:

>4 provinces, 1 territory*, and 1 capital territory**; Balochistan, Federally Administered Tribal Areas*, Islamabad Capital Territory**, Khyber Pakhtunkhwa (formerly North-West Frontier Province), Punjab, Sindh
>
>note: the Pakistani-administered portion of the disputed Jammu and Kashmir region consists of two administrative entities: Azad Kashmir and Gilgit-Baltistan

Independence:

>14 August 1947 (from British India)

National holiday:

Republic Day, 23 March (1956)

Constitution:

12 April 1973; suspended 5 July 1977, restored 30
December 1985; suspended 15 October 1999, restored in
stages in 2002; amended 31 December 2003; suspended 3
November 2007; restored 15 December 2007; last
amended 28 February 2012

Legal system:

common law system with Islamic law influence

International law organization participation:

accepts compulsory ICJ jurisdiction with reservations;
non-party state to the ICCt

Suffrage:

18 years of age; universal; note - there are joint electorates
and reserved parliamentary seats for women and non-
Muslims

Executive branch:

chief of state: President Asif Ali ZARDARI (since 9
September 2008)

head of government: Prime Minister Raja Pervaiz
ASHRAF (since 22 June 2012); Deputy Prime Minister
Chaudhry Pervais ELAHI (since 25 June 2012)

cabinet: Cabinet appointed by the president upon the
advice of the prime minister

elections: president elected by secret ballot through an
Electoral College comprising the members of the Senate,

National Assembly, and provincial assemblies for a five-year term; election last held on 6 September 2008 (next to be held not later than 2013); note - any person who is a Muslim and not less than 45 years of age and qualified to be elected as a member of the National Assembly can contest the presidential election; the prime minister selected by the National Assembly

election results: Asif Ali ZARDARI elected president; ZARDARI 481 votes, SIDDIQUE 153 votes, SYED 44 votes; Prime Minister Raja Pervais ASHRAF elected by Parliament - ASHRAF 211 votes, Sardar Mehtab ABBASI 89 votes

Legislative branch:

bicameral parliament or Majlis-e-Shoora consists of the Senate (104 seats; members indirectly elected by provincial assemblies and the territories' representatives in the National Assembly to serve six-year terms; one half are elected every three years) and the National Assembly (342 seats; 272 members elected by popular vote; 60 seats reserved for women; 10 seats reserved for non-Muslims; members serve five-year terms)

elections: Senate - last held on 2 March 2012 (next to be held in March 2015); National Assembly - last held on 18 February 2008 (next to be held in 2013)

election results: Senate - percent of vote by party - NA; seats by party - PPPP 41, PML-N 14, ANP 12, JUI-F 7,

MQM 7, PML-Q 5, BNP-A 4, NPP 1, PML-F 1,
independents 12; National Assembly - percent of votes by
party - NA; seats by party as of November 2012 - PPPP
125, PML-N 92, PML 50, MQM 24, ANP 13, JUI-F 8,
PML-F 5, BNP-A 1, NPP 1, PPP-S 1, independents 18,
unfilled seats - 4

Judicial branch:

Supreme Court (justices appointed by the president);
Federal Islamic or Sharia Court

Political parties and leaders:

Awami National Party or ANP [Asfandyar Wali KHAN];
Balochistan National Party-Awami or BNP-A; Balochistan
National Party-Hayee Group or BNP-H [Dr. Hayee
BALOCH]; Balochistan National Party-Mengal or BNP-
M; Jamaat-i Islami or JI [Syed Munawar HASAN];
Jamhoori Watan Party or JWP; Jamiat Ahle Hadith or JAH
[Sajid MIR]; Jamiat-i Ulema-i Islam Fazl-ur Rehman or
JUI-F [Fazl-ur REHMAN]; Jamiat-i Ulema-i Islam Sami-
ul HAQ or JUI-S [Sami ul-HAQ]; Jamiat-i Ulema-i
Pakistan or JUP [Abul Khair ZUBAIR]; Millat-e-Jafferia
[Allama Sajid NAQVI]; Muttahida Qaumi Movement or
MQM [Altaf HUSSAIN]; National Peoples Party or NPP;
Pakhtun-khwa Milli Awami Party or PKMAP [Mahmood
Khan ACHAKZAI]; Pakistan Awami Tehrik or PAT
[Tahir ul QADRI]; Pakistan Muslim League-Quaid-i
Azam or PML-Q [Chaudhry Shujaat HUSSAIN]; Pakistan

Muslim League-Functional or PML-F [Pir PAGARO]; Pakistan Muslim League-Nawaz or PML-N [Nawaz SHARIF]; Pakistan Peoples Party Parliamentarians or PPPP [Bilawal Bhutto ZARDARI, chairman; Asif Ali ZARDARI, co-chairman]; Quami Watan Party or QWP [Aftab Ahmed Khan SHERPAO]; Pakistan Tehrik-e Insaaf or PTI [Imran KHAN]

note: political alliances in Pakistan can shift frequently

Political pressure groups and leaders:

other: military (most important political force); ulema (clergy); landowners; industrialists; small merchants

International organization participation:

ADB, ARF, ASEAN (dialogue partner), C, CICA, CP, D-8, ECO, FAO, G-11, G-24, G-77, IAEA, IBRD, ICAO, ICC (national committees), ICRM, IDA, IDB, IFAD, IFC, IFRCS, IHO, ILO, IMF, IMO, IMSO, Interpol, IOC, IOM, IPU, ISO, ITSO, ITU, ITUC (NGOs), LAIA (observer), MIGA, MINURSO, MONUSCO, NAM, OAS (observer), OIC, OPCW, PCA, SAARC, SACEP, SCO (observer), UN, UNAMID, UNCTAD, UNESCO, UNHCR, UNIDO, UNISFA, UNMIL, UNMIT, UNOCI, UNSC (temporary), UNWTO, UPU, WCO, WFTU (NGOs), WHO, WIPO, WMO, WTO

Diplomatic representation in the US:

chief of mission: Ambassador Sheherbano "Sherry" REHMAN

chancery: 3517 International Court, Washington, DC 20008

telephone: [1] (202) 243-6500

FAX: [1] (202) 686-1544

consulate(s) general: Boston (Honorary Consulate General), Chicago, Houston, Los Angeles, New York

consulate(s): Chicago, Houston

Diplomatic representation from the US:

chief of mission: Ambassador Richard Olson

embassy: Diplomatic Enclave, Ramna 5, Islamabad

mailing address: 8100 Islamabad Pl., Washington, DC 20521-8100

telephone: [92] (51) 208-0000

FAX: [92] (51) 227-6427

consulate(s) general: Karachi

consulate(s): Lahore, Peshawar

Key Leaders:

Pres.	Asif Ali ZARDARI
Prime Min.	Raja Pervaiz ASHRAF
Dep. Prime Min.	Chaudhry Pervaiz ELAHI
Min. of Benazir Income Support Program	Farzana RAJA

Min. of Capital Admin. & Development	Nazar Muhammad GONDAL
Min. of Climate Change	Rana Muhammad Farooq Saeed KHAN
Min. of Commerce	Makhdoom Amin FAHIM
Min. of Communications	Arbab Alamgir KHAN
Min. of Defense	Syed Naveed QAMAR
Min. of Defense Production	Sardar Bahadur Ahmed Khan SIHAR
Min. of Economic Affairs & Statistics	Abdul Hafeez SHAIKH
Min. of Education & Training	Sheikh Waqqas AKRAM
Min. of Finance, Revenue, Planning, & Development	Saleem MANDVIWALLA
Min. of Foreign Affairs	Hina Rabbani KHAR
Min. of Housing	Sardar Talib Hassan NAKAI
Min. of Human	Chaudhry Wajahat

Resources Development	HUSSAIN
Min. of Human Rights	
Min. of Industries	Chaudhry Pervaiz ELAHI
Min. of Information & Broadcasting	Qamar Zaman KAIRA
Min. of Interior	A. Rehman MALIK
Min. of Interprovinical Coordination	Mir Hazar Khan BIJARANI
Min. of Kashmir Affairs & Gilgit-Baltistan	Mian Manzoor Ahmad WATTOO
Min. of Law & Justice	Farooq Hamid NAEK
Min. of Narcotics Control	Haji Khuda Bux RAJAR
Min. of National Food Security & Research	Mir Israr Ullah ZEHRI
Min. of National Harmony	
Min. of National	Samina Khalid

Heritage & Integration	GHURKI
Min. of National Regulations & Services	Firdous Ashiq AWAN
Min. of Overseas Pakistanis	Muhammad Farooq SATTAR
Min. of Parliamentary Affairs	Farooq Hamid NAEK
Min. of Petroleum & Natural Resources	
Min. of Political Affairs	Moula Bakhsh CHANDIO
Min. of Ports & Shipping	Baber Khan GHAURI
Min. of Postal Services	Sardar Al Haj Muhammad Umar GORGAGE
Min. of Privatization	Ghous Bux Khan MAHER
Min. for Production	Chaudhry Anwar Ali CHEEMA
Min. of Railways	Haji Ghulam Ahmed BILOUR

Min. of Religious Affairs	Syed Khursheed SHAH
Min. of Science & Technology	Mir Changez Khan JAMALI
Min. of States & Frontier Regions (SAFRON)	Shaukat ULLAH
Min. of Textile Industry	Makhdoom SHAHABUDDIN
Min. of Water & Power	Chaudhry Ahmed MUKHTAR
Min. of Works	Chaudhry Liaqat Abbas BHATTI
Governor, State Bank of Pakistan	Yaseen ANWAR
Ambassador to the US	Sheherbano REHMAN
Permanent Representative to the UN, New York	Masood KHAN

Flag description:

green with a vertical white band (symbolizing the role of religious minorities) on the hoist side; a large white crescent and star are centered in the green field; the crescent, star, and color green are traditional symbols of Islam

National symbol(s):

star and crescent

National anthem:

<u>name</u>: "Qaumi Tarana" (National Anthem)

<u>lyrics/music</u>: Abu-Al-Asar Hafeez JULLANDHURI/Ahmed Ghulamali CHAGLA

<u>note</u>: adopted 1954; the anthem is also known as "Pak sarzamin shad bad" (Blessed Be the Sacred Land)

Chapter 5: Economy

Economy - overview:

Decades of internal political disputes and low levels of foreign investment have led to slow growth and underdevelopment in Pakistan. Agriculture accounts for more than one-fifth of output and two-fifths of employment. Textiles account for most of Pakistan's export earnings, and Pakistan's failure to expand a viable export base for other manufactures has left the country vulnerable to shifts in world demand. Official unemployment is under 6%, but this fails to capture the true picture, because much of the economy is informal and underemployment remains high. Over the past few years, low growth and high inflation, led by a spurt in food prices, have increased the amount of poverty - the UN Human Development Report estimated poverty in 2011 at almost 50% of the population. Inflation has worsened the situation, climbing from 7.7% in 2007 to almost 12% for 2011, before declining to 10% in 2012. As a result of political and economic instability, the Pakistani rupee has depreciated more than 40% since 2007. The government agreed to an International Monetary Fund Standby Arrangement in November 2008 in response to a balance of payments crisis. Although the economy has stabilized since the crisis, it has failed to recover. Foreign investment has not returned, due to investor concerns related to governance, energy, security, and a slow-down in the global economy. Remittances from overseas workers, averaging about $1 billion a month since March 2011, remain a bright spot for Pakistan. However, after a small current account surplus in fiscal year 2011 (July 2010/June 2011), Pakistan's current account turned to deficit in fiscal year 2012, spurred by higher prices for imported oil and lower prices for exported cotton. Pakistan remains stuck in a low-income, low-growth trap, with growth averaging about 3% per year from 2008 to 2012. Pakistan must address long standing issues related to government revenues and energy production in order to spur the amount of economic growth that will be necessary to employ its growing population. Other long term challenges include expanding investment in education and healthcare, and reducing dependence on foreign donors.

GDP (purchasing power parity):

$514.6 billion (2012 est.)

country comparison to the world: 28

$496.3 billion (2011 est.)

$481.7 billion (2010 est.)

note: data are in 2012 US dollars

GDP (official exchange rate):

$230.5 billion (2012 est.)

GDP - real growth rate:

3.7% (2012 est.)

country comparison to the world: 93

3% (2011 est.)

3.1% (2010 est.)

GDP - per capita (PPP):

$2,900 (2012 est.)

country comparison to the world: 175

$2,800 (2011 est.)

$2,800 (2010 est.)

note: data are in 2012 US dollars

GDP - composition by sector:

agriculture: 20.1%

industry: 25.5%

services: 54.4% (2012 est.)

Labor force:

60.36 million

country comparison to the world: 10

note: extensive export of labor, mostly to the Middle East, and use of child labor (2012 est.)

Labor force - by occupation:

agriculture: 45.1%

industry: 20.7%

services: 34.2% (2010 est.)

Unemployment rate:

5.6% (2012 est.)

country comparison to the world: 55

5.6% (2011 est.)

note: substantial underemployment exists

Population below poverty line:

22.3% (FY05/06 est.)

Household income or consumption by percentage share:

lowest 10%: 9.9%

highest 10%: 39.3% (FY07/08)

Distribution of family income - Gini index:

30.6 (FY07/08)

country comparison to the world: 114

41 (FY98/99)

Investment (gross fixed):

10.9% of GDP (2012 est.)

country comparison to the world: 146

Budget:

revenues: $29.51 billion

expenditures: $44.19 billion (2012 est.)

Taxes and other revenues:

12.8% of GDP (2012 est.)

country comparison to the world: 201

Budget surplus (+) or deficit (-):

-6.4% of GDP (2012 est.)

country comparison to the world: 179

Public debt:

50.4% of GDP (2012 est.)

country comparison to the world: 62

60.1% of GDP (2011 est.)

Inflation rate (consumer prices):

11.3% (2012 est.)

country comparison to the world: 201

11.9% (2011 est.)

Central bank discount rate:

12% (31 January 2012 est.)

country comparison to the world: 12

14% (31 December 2010 est.)

Commercial bank prime lending rate:

12.2% (31 December 2012 est.)

country comparison to the world: 56

14.12% (31 December 2011 est.)

Stock of narrow money:

$60.68 billion (31 December 2012 est.)

country comparison to the world: 44

$56.34 billion (31 December 2011 est.)

Stock of broad money:

$76.16 billion (31 December 2011 est.)

country comparison to the world: 59

$71.36 billion (31 December 2010 est.)

Stock of domestic credit:

$92.06 billion (31 December 2012 est.)

country comparison to the world: 55

$86.19 billion (31 December 2011 est.)

Market value of publicly traded shares:

$32.76 billion (31 December 2011)

country comparison to the world: 54

$38.17 billion (31 December 2010)

$33.24 billion (31 December 2009)

Agriculture - products:

cotton, wheat, rice, sugarcane, fruits, vegetables; milk, beef, mutton, eggs

Industries:

textiles and apparel, food processing, pharmaceuticals, construction materials, paper products, fertilizer, shrimp

Industrial production growth rate:

3% (2011 est.)

country comparison to the world: 102

Current account balance:

-$4.632 billion (2012 est.)

country comparison to the world: 163

$268 million (2011 est.)

Exports:

$24.66 billion (2012 est.)

country comparison to the world: 71

$26.3 billion (2011 est.)

Exports - commodities:

textiles (garments, bed linen, cotton cloth, yarn), rice, leather goods, sports goods, chemicals, manufactures, carpets and rugs

Exports - partners:

US 15%, UAE 9.7%, Afghanistan 9.5%, China 9.2%, UK 5%, Germany 4.5% (2012 est.)

Imports:

$40.82 billion (2012 est.)

country comparison to the world: 61

$38.93 billion (2011 est.)

Imports - commodities:

petroleum, petroleum products, machinery, plastics, transportation equipment, edible oils, paper and paperboard, iron and steel, tea

Imports - partners:

UAE 17.2%, China 15%, Saudi Arabia 11.2%, Kuwait 8.9%, Malaysia 5.4%, Japan 4.3% (2012 est.)

Reserves of foreign exchange and gold:

$13.5 billion (30 November 2012 est.)

country comparison to the world: 68

$18.09 billion (31 December 2011 est.)

Debt - external:

$55.98 billion (31 December 2012 est.)

country comparison to the world: 57

$58.27 billion (31 December 2011 est.)

Stock of direct foreign investment - at home:

$22.38 billion (31 December 2012 est.)

country comparison to the world: 69

$21.88 billion (31 December 2011 est.)

Stock of direct foreign investment - abroad:

$1.482 billion (31 December 2012 est.)

country comparison to the world: 72

$1.432 billion (31 December 2011 est.)

Exchange rates:

Pakistani rupees (PKR) per US dollar -

95.1 (2012 est.)

86.3434 (2011 est.)

85.194 (2010 est.)

81.71 (2009)

70.64 (2008)

Fiscal year:

1 July - 30 June

Chapter 6: Energy

Electricity - production:

    94.65 billion kWh (2011 est.)

    country comparison to the world: 35

Electricity - consumption:

    70.1 billion kWh (2011 est.)

    country comparison to the world: 39

Electricity - exports:

    0 kWh (2011 est.)

    country comparison to the world: 117

Electricity - imports:

    0 kWh (2010 est.)

    country comparison to the world: 120

Electricity - installed generating capacity:

    20.2 million kW (2009 est.)

    country comparison to the world: 36

Electricity - from fossil fuels:

    65.2% of total installed capacity (2009 est.)

    country comparison to the world: 128

Electricity - from nuclear fuels:

    2.3% of total installed capacity (2009 est.)

    country comparison to the world: 27

Electricity - from hydroelectric plants:

    32.5% of total installed capacity (2009 est.)

    country comparison to the world: 66

Electricity - from other renewable sources:

0% of total installed capacity (2009 est.)

country comparison to the world: 174

Crude oil - production:

63,080 bbl/day (2011 est.)

country comparison to the world: 55

Crude oil - exports:

0 bbl/day (2009 est.)

country comparison to the world: 168

Crude oil - imports:

183,000 bbl/day (2009 est.)

country comparison to the world: 36

Crude oil - proved reserves:

480.9 million bbl (1 January 2013 est.)

country comparison to the world: 52

Refined petroleum products - production:

215,900 bbl/day (2008 est.)

country comparison to the world: 52

Refined petroleum products - consumption:

426,700 bbl/day (2011 est.)

country comparison to the world: 35

Refined petroleum products - exports:

26,830 bbl/day (2008 est.)

country comparison to the world: 70

Refined petroleum products - imports:

195,700 bbl/day (2008 est.)

Natural gas - production:

42.9 billion cu m (2011 est.)

country comparison to the world: 23

Natural gas - consumption:

42.9 billion cu m (2011 est.)

country comparison to the world: 24

Natural gas - exports:

0 cu m (2010 est.)

country comparison to the world: 132

Natural gas - imports:

0 cu m (2010 est.)

country comparison to the world: 117

Natural gas - proved reserves:

753.8 billion cu m (1 January 2012 est.)

country comparison to the world: 30

Carbon dioxide emissions from consumption of energy:

151.6 million Mt (2010 est.)

country comparison to the world: 34

Chapter 7: Communications

Telephones - main lines in use:

> 5.722 million (2011)
>
> <u>country comparison to the world</u>: 30

Telephones - mobile cellular:

> 111 million (2011)
>
> <u>country comparison to the world</u>: 9

Telephone system:

> <u>general assessment</u>: the telecommunications infrastructure
> is improving dramatically with foreign and domestic
> investments in fixed-line and mobile-cellular networks;
> system consists of microwave radio relay, coaxial cable,
> fiber-optic cable, cellular, and satellite networks;
> <u>domestic</u>: mobile-cellular subscribership has skyrocketed,
> exceeding 110 million by the end of 2011, up from only
> about 300,000 in 2000; more than 90 percent of Pakistanis
> live within areas that have cell phone coverage and more
> than half of all Pakistanis have access to a cell phone; fiber
> systems are being constructed throughout the country to
> aid in network growth; fixed line availability has risen
> only marginally over the same period and there are still
> difficulties getting fixed-line service to rural areas
> <u>international</u>: country code - 92; landing point for the
> SEA-ME-WE-3 and SEA-ME-WE-4 submarine cable
> systems that provide links to Asia, the Middle East, and

Europe; satellite earth stations - 3 Intelsat (1 Atlantic Ocean and 2 Indian Ocean); 3 operational international gateway exchanges (1 at Karachi and 2 at Islamabad); microwave radio relay to neighboring countries

Broadcast media:

media is government regulated; 1 dominant state-owned TV broadcaster, Pakistan Television Corporation (PTV), operates a network consisting of 5 channels; private TV broadcasters are permitted; to date 69 foreign satellite channels are operational; the state-owned radio network operates more than 40 stations; nearly 100 commercially-licensed privately-owned radio stations provide programming mostly limited to music and talk shows (2007)

Internet country code:

.pk

Internet hosts:

365,813 (2012)

country comparison to the world: 57

Internet users:

20.431 million (2009)

country comparison to the world: 20

Chapter 8: Transportation

Airports:

> 151 (2012)

> country comparison to the world: 37

Airports - with paved runways:

> total: 107

> over 3,047 m: 15

> 2,438 to 3,047 m: 20

> 1,524 to 2,437 m: 42

> 914 to 1,523 m: 20

> under 914 m: 10 (2012)

Airports - with unpaved runways:

> total: 44

> 1,524 to 2,437 m: 11

> 914 to 1,523 m: 9

> under 914 m: 24 (2012)

Heliports:

> 24 (2012)

Pipelines:

> gas 10,514 km; oil 2,013 km; refined products 787 km
> (2010)

Railways:

> total: 7,791 km

> country comparison to the world: 27

broad gauge: 7,479 km 1.676-m gauge (293 km electrified)

narrow gauge: 312 km 1.000-m gauge (2007)

Roadways:

total: 260,760 km

country comparison to the world: 20

paved: 180,910 km (includes 711 km of expressways)

unpaved: 79,850 km (2007)

Merchant marine:

total: 11

country comparison to the world: 111

by type: bulk carrier 5, cargo 3, petroleum tanker 3

registered in other countries: 11 (Comoros 5, Marshall Islands 1, Moldova 1, Panama 3, Saint Kitts and Nevis 1) (2010)

Ports and terminals:

Karachi, Port Muhammad Bin Qasim

Chapter 9: Military

Military branches:

Pakistan Army (includes National Guard), Pakistan Navy (includes Marines and Maritime Security Agency), Pakistan Air Force (Pakistan Fiza'ya) (2010)

Military service age and obligation:

17-23 years of age for voluntary military service; soldiers cannot be deployed for combat until age 18; the Pakistani Air Force and Pakistani Navy have inducted their first female pilots and sailors; service obligation (Navy) 10-18 years; retirement required after 18-30 years service or age 40-52 (2012)

Manpower available for military service:

males age 16-49: 48,453,305

females age 16-49: 44,898,096 (2010 est.)

Manpower fit for military service:

males age 16-49: 37,945,440

females age 16-49: 37,381,549 (2010 est.)

Manpower reaching militarily significant age annually:

male: 2,237,723

female: 2,104,906 (2010 est.)

Military expenditures:

3% of GDP (2007 est.)

country comparison to the world: 41

Chapter 10: Transnational Issues

Disputes - international:

various talks and confidence-building measures cautiously have begun to defuse tensions over Kashmir, particularly since the October 2005 earthquake in the region; Kashmir nevertheless remains the site of the world's largest and most militarized territorial dispute with portions under the de facto administration of China (Aksai Chin), India (Jammu and Kashmir), and Pakistan (Azad Kashmir and Northern Areas); UN Military Observer Group in India and Pakistan has maintained a small group of peacekeepers since 1949; India does not recognize Pakistan's ceding historic Kashmir lands to China in 1964; India and Pakistan have maintained their 2004 cease-fire in Kashmir and initiated discussions on defusing the armed standoff in the Siachen glacier region; Pakistan protests India's fencing the highly militarized Line of Control and construction of the Baglihar Dam on the Chenab River in Jammu and Kashmir, which is part of the larger dispute on water sharing of the Indus River and its tributaries; to defuse tensions and prepare for discussions on a maritime boundary, India and Pakistan seek technical resolution of the disputed boundary in Sir Creek estuary at the mouth of the Rann of Kutch in the Arabian Sea; Pakistani maps continue to show the Junagadh claim in India's Gujarat

State; by 2005, Pakistan, with UN assistance, repatriated 2.3 million Afghan refugees leaving slightly more than a million, many of whom remain at their own choosing; Pakistan has sent troops across and built fences along some remote tribal areas of its treaty-defined Durand Line border with Afghanistan, which serve as bases for foreign terrorists and other illegal activities; Afghan, Coalition, and Pakistan military meet periodically to clarify the alignment of the boundary on the ground and on maps

Refugees and internally displaced persons:

refugees (country of origin): 1,701,945 (Afghanistan) (2011)

IDPs: 774,594 (figure only includes IDPs in Federally Administered Tribal Areas (FATA) and Khyber-Pakhtunkwa; fighting in the FATA, Khyber-Pakhtunkwa, and Balochistan since 2004; military operations in SWAT in 2009; earthquakes and floods) (2012)

Illicit drugs:

significant transit area for Afghan drugs, including heroin, opium, morphine, and hashish, bound for Iran, Western markets, the Gulf States, Africa, and Asia; financial crimes related to drug trafficking, terrorism, corruption, and smuggling remain problems; opium poppy cultivation estimated to be 2,300 hectares in 2007 with 600 of those hectares eradicated; federal and provincial authorities continue to conduct anti-poppy campaigns that utilizes forced eradication, fines, and arrests

Other Key Facts™ Titles

Key Facts on Syria

Key Facts on China

Key Facts on Qatar

Key Facts on India

Key Facts on Germany

Key Facts on Argentina

Key Facts on Russia

Key Facts on North Korea

Key Facts on Brazil

Key Facts on Italy

Key Facts on the United Arab Emirates

Key Facts on the European Union

Key Facts on Pakistan

Key Facts on Saudi Arabia

Key Facts on Cyprus

Key Facts on Iran

Key Facts on Afghanistan

Key Facts on Iraq

Key Facts on Indonesia

Key Facts on South Korea

All Key Facts™ Titles are

Available at www.Amazon.com

THE INTERNATIONALIST®

2013

www.internationalist.com

www.ingramcontent.com/pod-product-compliance
Lightning Source LLC
Chambersburg PA
CBHW051256170526
45165CB00004B/1741